Follow One Course Until Success

by

Sakshi Chamat

Gyanvriksha Publications
ज्ञानोद्याने, पुस्तकं सर्वं बीजम्

First Edition: March 2024

Design by Gyanvriksha Publications
Cover photography by Sakshi chamat

Gyanvriksha Publications
gyanvrikshapublications@gmail.com

Printed in Bharat (INDIA)

"Although having a built-in survival mechanism is fortunate, an excess of pain and worry can diminish life's quality. Fortunately, you have the ability to transform your perspective. Harnessing the power of our powerful minds, we can reshape our perception of the world, infusing it with positivity. This book is your guide to understanding and implementing these transformative mental shifts."

"MASTERING POSITIVITY: A PRACTICAL GUIDE TO OVERCOME NEGATIVITY AND BETTER MANAGE YOUR FEELINGS"

Introduction: About the Book

In the expansive realm of literature exploring the intricacies of human emotions, "FOCUS" emerges as a guiding light, offering readers a profound and comprehensive understanding of the emotional landscape. While countless books touch upon the subject of feelings and their impact, this book distinguishes itself by providing a complete picture of the origins, purposes, and significant influence emotions wield over our lives.

Within the pages of "FOCUS," emotions are likened to tricky wizards, capable of casting spells that sometimes ensnare us in their intricate webs. The narrative underscores the notion that emotions play a pivotal role in shaping the trajectory of our lives. Failure to comprehend these emotional wizards can act as a barrier, preventing us from realizing and creating the life we authentically desire.

This book serves as a guide for those grappling with challenging feelings or seeking a deeper understanding of emotional dynamics. By the journey's end, readers will not only unravel the mysteries of emotions but also gain valuable insights and practical strategies to effectively navigate and harness these potent forces for personal growth.

"FOCUS" is an invitation to embark on a transformative exploration—a journey that promises a nuanced comprehension of emotions, empowering individuals to not only decipher the spells of their emotional wizards but also to utilize these insights for personal development and the creation of a life filled with purpose and fulfilment.

"This book encompasses various aspects. While I don't anticipate you'll explore every detail, I encourage you to choose and implement some in your life. Keep in mind that the outcomes derived from this book correlate with the time and effort you invest. If you think this book could be helpful to your family or friends, do share it with them. Emotions are intricate, and I believe we can all benefit from a deeper comprehension of this subject."

Contents

Powerful Focus:

Build strong focus on your work:

Fear can be like a roadblock that keeps us from reaching our goals and dreams. Sometimes, we believe that only a chosen few can achieve greatness, that they're just lucky. But the truth is, those who have accomplished their goals made a decision to believe in themselves. Life is all about the choices we make, and giving in to fear is one of them.

Let's not waste any more time. It's time to take action. It's time to conquer our fears. Let's make the decision to:

1. Lead, not Follow:

Instead of just going along with what everyone else is doing, take charge. Be a leader in your own life. Make decisions that align with your goals and values.

2. Create, not Consume:

Don't just be a passive observer of life. Create something. Whether it's art, ideas, or solutions, contribute to the world around you instead of just consuming what others have created.

3. Stay Positive, not Negative:

It's easy to focus on the negatives, but choose to see the positive side of things. A positive mindset can make a significant difference in how you approach challenges and opportunities.

4. Solve Problems, not Complain:

Complaining doesn't solve anything. Instead of dwelling on problems, focus on finding solutions. Take a proactive approach to challenges, and you'll find yourself making progress.

Life is full of choices, and it's up to us to decide which path to take. Let's not let fear hold us back. Instead, let's embrace the power of our decisions and work towards the life we want. The journey starts now.

Choose joy over melancholy, and let your strength shine through instead of feeling weak. Make the decision to dare to do whatever you want. Say no to a life filled with stress, anxiety, pain, hurt, and sadness. Embrace a life filled with joy and free from fear.

Don't underestimate yourself by thinking it's impossible to live fearlessly. We often fall into the misconception that some people are born leaders, millionaires, or artists. The truth is, these successful individuals have learned how to overcome obstacles and live fulfilling lives. It's not about being born with a certain trait; it's about developing the mindset and skills needed to navigate challenges.

When you believe that living fearlessly is out of reach, you limit your own potential. Break free from this limiting belief. Understand that overcoming obstacles is a skill that can be learned and honed over time. Embracing challenges, rather than avoiding them, is the key to a fulfilling life.

Living without fear doesn't mean a life without challenges. It means facing challenges with courage and resilience. It means acknowledging that setbacks are part of the journey but not the end of it. Successful people embrace difficulties as opportunities for growth and learning.

So, let's redefine success. It's not about being born with a silver spoon or inherent talents. Success is about facing fears, overcoming obstacles, and creating a life that brings you joy. It's about making choices that align with your values and aspirations. Today, decide to live a life filled with joy, strength, and fearlessness. You have the power to shape your own narrative and create a fulfilling life.

Navigating Life's Challenges: A Journey to Resilience and Fulfillment

Life can be incredibly tough – no denying that. Anyone who doesn't recognize this is either out of touch with reality or has had an exceptionally privileged upbringing. Most of us don't fall into those categories, so we have to face life's challenges head-on.

Here's a thought: to lead a happy and satisfying life, you don't need to conquer life completely. You just need to be a little tougher than it is. When work, politics, relationships, health issues, and various problems try to bring you down, dig deep and endure just one step more. Life may throw challenge after challenge at you, but remember, you have the strength to face it.

It's easy to feel overwhelmed when life gets tough. The constant barrage of issues can make us want to give up, question our purpose, and wonder why we bother getting out of bed each morning. But here's the reality: there is no alternative. We can't escape life's challenges, so the only way forward is to keep going.

Winning the battles within ourselves is the key. When we overcome our inner struggles, we gather the energy needed to confront life head-on. It's a journey that takes time, filled with ups and downs, but the long-term rewards are worth the effort.

Acknowledging the difficulties we face is the first step. Instead of surrendering mentally, we can choose to stay focused and mentally strong. Yes, life is hard, but our response to it can make all the difference. When we triumph over our inner battles, we unlock the power to tackle whatever life throws our way. So, let's face life with determination, knowing that we have the resilience to navigate its challenges and find fulfillment along the way.

The Lasting Impact of Winning Inner Battles

I was genuinely surprised to find that the principles outlined in "Win Your Inner Battles" continue to stand strong. Witnessing the long-term effects of embracing this way of life has been nothing short of amazing. Unlike those who advocate for the "fake it till you make it" approach, I've always been a proponent of honesty and authenticity—it's just in my nature.

When I penned this book, I stayed true to my values, maintaining honesty throughout. I firmly believe that, before venturing into any aspect of life, one must address their internal struggles. This belief still holds true for me. Amidst the plethora of life and business advice circulating, I stand by the conviction that resolving your inner conflicts is the foundational step for any meaningful endeavor.

The Vital Link Between Mental Fitness and a Fulfilling Life

Ensuring your mental well-being is crucial for leading a satisfying life. While achieving external goals like running a marathon, getting a promotion, or making money in the stock market may bring success, it doesn't guarantee genuine satisfaction if your mental state is neglected. I've observed numerous individuals, inherently kind, talented, and good, succumb to depression despite their positive qualities. They don't deserve to carry the weight of sadness or constantly exist in what I term a "funeral mood," a state of mind marred by negativity.

Take a moment to reflect on your own life. Feeling consistently bad about yourself is not normal. A typical person may experience occasional fatigue or a brief period of feeling down, but they usually bounce back after a good night's sleep. Such moments might occur a few times a year. However, if you find yourself in a constant cycle of ups and downs, it's a sign that your mental well-being needs attention.

Navigating Life's Challenges: Overcoming Anxiety and Embracing Growth

Feeling anxious about the unknown is a common human experience. Simultaneously, many of us yearn for a deeper sense of fulfillment and become frustrated when our lives feel lacking. True happiness, however, isn't tied to our social status or income level; it stems from personal progress and development.

Yet, constant inner conflict stifles our potential for growth. Those who've attained personal success or happiness have learned to surmount their obstacles. Instead of resigning ourselves to limitations with statements like "I'm just not that type of person," we must recognize that every aspect of life is a skill that can be learned.

Conquering our inner adversaries is crucial, but it's essential to acknowledge that a life without fear is unattainable. To advance in life, we must confront our fears head-on, embracing them as opportunities for growth. It's a continual journey; everyone experiences fear, but it's how we face it that defines our progress.

Confronting Your Fears: Unlocking the Path to a Fulfilling Life

What keeps you up at night? Is it the thought of ending a relationship, making tough decisions, facing solitude, navigating intimacy, contemplating a career change, fearing failure, or worrying about what others think of you? Each person on this planet possesses the potential for a good life, blessed with unique talents and gifts. This isn't just empty encouragement; it's a truth often hindered by the formidable force of fear.

Our fears, be they of relationships, decisions, loneliness, intimacy, career shifts, failure, or judgment, can become stumbling blocks on the path to pursuing our talents and dreams. It's not a shortage of resources that holds us back, but rather a lack of confidence. Overcoming fear is the key to unlocking the immense potential within, propelling us toward a life rich with the pursuit of our passions and the realization of our dreams.

Breaking Free: The Power of Conquering Fear in Today's World

In our interconnected world, the pressure to conform to societal norms is more prevalent than ever. Sadly, many individuals with incredible talents carry their gifts to the grave due to the fear of pursuing their dreams. This fear often stems from societal expectations and the lessons ingrained in us by others.

From a young age, we are conditioned to follow a conventional life path: blend in, pursue education, secure a stable job, get married, and buy a house. This prescribed route is so deeply ingrained that deviating from it is often met with terror. For instance, staying in a job you dislike can lead to constant stress, affecting your mood, ambition, and, most significantly, your health. The consequences of stress on our bodies are severe, yet many spend their lives evading their fears.

Conquering fear is not only liberating but also rejuvenating. The newfound freedom grants you the energy to contribute positively to the lives of those you love. The encouraging news is that overcoming fear is a simple skill, one that can significantly transform your life.

Art of Fear Mastery: A Practical Approach

Mastering the skill of conquering fear is akin to honing any other ability – it requires consistent practice and the right set of tools. It all begins with a crucial realization: fear is a choice. Research indicates that a significant 65% of our thoughts tend to be negative, making it a considerable challenge to maintain a positive mindset in today's world. It's almost as if staying optimistic requires a full-time commitment.

Today's media landscape amplifies this challenge. Turning on the TV or opening a news app bombards us with fear-inducing messages instantly. Whether it's news of a struggling economy, tragic events, or companies facing challenges, the overall tone of news tends to be negative. While this negativity is understandable, it underscores the importance of actively choosing how we engage with and respond to the information presented to us.

Empowering Ourselves: Taking Control Amidst Life's Challenges

Life is not always picture-perfect, and it's crucial to acknowledge that not every situation is ideal. However, one undeniable truth stands out: our current circumstances are not solely dictated by external factors. Despite the unpredictability of life, we have the power to shape our responses and actions. It's perplexing why we allow external circumstances, such as fear of economic downturns, traffic accidents, or potential threats, to wield such influence over our lives.

In reality, we don't have control over these external events. What we can control, though, are our actions and how we choose to navigate the challenges life throws our way. By recognizing this distinction, we empower ourselves to maintain agency over our lives, irrespective of the external circumstances that may surround us.

Understanding Fear: A Path to Wisdom and Self-Mastery

"Fear is the main source of superstition and one of the main sources of cruelty." - Bertrand Russell

Perhaps you find yourself fearing public speaking, ending a relationship, confronting your boss, job loss, financial setbacks, asking someone on a date, or even a routine dentist visit. The spectrum of common fears is vast, but what matters most is not the specific fear itself. It's crucial to recognize that feeling fear is entirely natural. Everyone experiences it, but the key lies in understanding why we feel fear. This understanding is essential because awareness is the first step towards resolving any challenge.

Fear, as Bertrand Russell suggests, serves as a primary source of superstition and cruelty. However, its fundamental purpose is rooted in evolution: to warn us of potential danger and trigger a fight or flight response. While our modern lives may not mirror the threats faced in early civilizations, the fear mechanism remains ingrained in our brains, originating from the reptilian part of our mind.

In the context of our contemporary, relatively safe lives, fear often becomes a hindrance rather than a protector. The threats we encounter today are incomparable to the challenges of our hunter-gatherer ancestors. Over millennia, civilization has made life progressively more comfortable, yet our brains still respond to perceived threats with the same intensity as if facing physical danger.

Recognizing that our fear response is outdated is crucial. Despite the ease of modern life, our brains struggle to distinguish between genuine physical threats and self-constructed fears. The key to overcoming fear is understanding its sensations, as this knowledge forms the basis for effectively confronting and conquering this internal adversary. In essence, it's a battle within ourselves that requires self-awareness, wisdom, and the realization that fear, once a protector, can become our most formidable foe.

Arm Yourself with Self-Knowledge: A Tactical Approach to Conquer Your Inner Enemy

Sun Tzu, the renowned military strategist, wisely said, "If you know the enemy and know yourself, you need not fear the result of a hundred battles." This ancient wisdom holds true in the battlefield of the mind, where self-awareness is your greatest weapon against the inner enemy. Understanding oneself is the key to victory over the challenges we face within.

To aid you in this journey of self-discovery, I've compiled a list of twenty questions designed to enhance your self-awareness. By answering these questions honestly, you'll gain valuable insights into your thoughts, feelings, and motivations. Armed with this self-knowledge, you can navigate the battles within and emerge victorious over your inner adversary.

1. What are my core values?

2. What motivates me to take action?

3. What are my greatest strengths?

4. What are my most significant weaknesses?

5. How do I handle stress and adversity?

6. What brings me a sense of fulfillment and joy?

7. What are my long-term goals?

8. How do I cope with failure or setbacks?

9. What fears hold me back from pursuing my dreams?

10. How do I prioritize my time and energy?

11. What kind of relationships do I value most?

12. How do I handle criticism or feedback?

13. What role does self-discipline play in my life?

14. What habits contribute to my well-being?

15. How do I define success for myself?

16. What lessons have I learned from past mistakes?

17. How do I recharge and maintain my mental health?

18. What limits do I place on my own potential?

19. How do I contribute positively to others' lives?

20. What steps can I take to continually improve myself?

By delving into these questions, you'll build a robust foundation of self-awareness, empowering yourself to face the battles within and emerge triumphant in the ongoing quest for personal growth and fulfillment.

Unleashing True Freedom: Navigating a World of Choices

Imagine waking up every morning and deciding exactly what you want to do, free from unwanted obligations and stress. Living a life of freedom isn't just a fantasy; it's an achievable reality in our ever-evolving world. Advancements in technology grant us the ability to work remotely and access unlimited information, enhancing our lives. However, despite these advancements, many of us find ourselves entangled in the web of obligations, debt, and societal expectations.

While the world becomes increasingly interconnected, the pursuit of success often feels like chasing an elusive dream without a clear definition. For me, success boils down to one fundamental principle: the freedom to live life on your terms without causing harm to others. True success, or freedom, isn't defined by job status, luxurious possessions, a model-like appearance, extravagant vacations, or a grandiose residence.

Contrary to those who oversimplify the path to freedom, achieving it requires more than just positive thinking. Freedom comes at a cost, but it's a cost worth paying. It involves making practical choices, navigating through challenges, and embracing a mindset that aligns with your authentic desires. As we traverse the journey towards genuine freedom, let us explore the nuanced reality of what it means to live a life of choice and autonomy.

Practical Paths to Freedom: Navigating Life on Your Terms

In the pursuit of freedom, there's no denying that money plays a crucial role. This book is designed to be highly practical, encompassing all the steps I've taken to attain the freedom I enjoy today. While my personal definition of freedom may differ from yours, the core principle remains universal: the ability to live life on your own terms.

It's important to acknowledge that, despite a shared desire for freedom, the specifics of what each person wants can vary significantly. This diversity in individual aspirations adds depth and complexity to the journey toward freedom. As we embark on this practical exploration, the book aims to provide tangible insights and actionable steps, recognizing that the path to freedom is unique for each person.

Whether your version of freedom aligns closely with mine or takes a different form, the practical strategies outlined in this book are intended to serve as a versatile guide, offering a roadmap to help you achieve the freedom you seek in your own life.

Breaking Free: Embracing Your Authentic Desires on the Path to True Freedom

One crucial lesson on the journey to freedom: don't harbor guilt for desiring what truly matters to you. Too often, external pressures lead us to adopt others' aspirations, be it our parents' expectations for our careers or the expectations set by our intimate relationships. The desire to please can lead us down paths that don't align with our authentic selves, jeopardizing our individuality.

Consider the pressure to pursue a career chosen by others, like becoming a doctor to meet your parents' expectations. Despite the lack of personal interest, you may find yourself on a path you never envisioned simply to appease others. Similarly, in intimate relationships, bending to the expectations of a partner can lead to actions that compromise your true self, eroding your character and sense of freedom.

This pattern extends to our financial lives, where many of us fall into the trap of overspending, accumulating debt, and working jobs we despise to sustain a lifestyle we don't even enjoy. How did we arrive at a point where every aspect of our lives feels alien? The daily grind is filled with unwelcome obligations, leaving us feeling trapped and miserable.

This book aims to guide you in rediscovering your authentic desires, breaking free from external pressures, and creating a life that truly aligns with who you are. It's time to escape the confines of someone else's expectations, reclaim control over your choices, and embark on a journey towards genuine freedom and fulfillment.

The Price of Freedom: Navigating Challenges on the Road to True Liberation

Freedom is the ultimate solution to the challenges we face, but let's be clear: it comes at a cost. Choosing to live life on your terms requires voluntary suffering. Others might disapprove, and some may even distance themselves from you. It involves doing the hard things that many avoid. Yet, on the other side of this voluntary suffering lies true freedom—a destination only a few dare to reach.

Consider the practical concerns that may arise: paying rent, managing student debt, credit card debt, and car loans. I've been there, facing the traps that easily snare us in financial burdens. Similar entanglements happen in romantic relationships, where two people might grow apart, leading to energy-draining dynamics. Despite these challenges, staying together or assuming that buying a house and having kids will fix everything only perpetuates the dissatisfaction.

Often, we find ourselves moving forward in life, but deep down, the desire to live authentically lingers. Unhappily, we remain confined because, as free as the world around us may be, we feel unfree. The realization hits that there's always a choice, a way out. Recognizing that we've willingly chosen a life that doesn't align with our true desires forces us to confront the uncomfortable truth. No matter who you are or where you find yourself, the innate desire for freedom persists within all of us. It's time to acknowledge it, embrace the challenges, and embark on a journey towards authentic liberation.

Embracing Solitude: A Path to Self-Strengthening and Inner Freedom

During times of solitude, we often find ourselves strengthening the core of our being. This notion of self is deeply rooted in Eastern philosophy and mindfulness practices. Central to this philosophy is the idea of transcending the incessant focus on oneself and living in a state of freedom beyond the dictates of desires and fears. This is the essence of Nirvana or Nibbana, representing a mind free from the sway of both pleasant and unpleasant sensations.

Human nature tends to gravitate toward two primary behaviors: the avoidance of unpleasant experiences and the pursuit of pleasurable feelings. As life calms down and we are left alone with our thoughts, we naturally seek to escape the unpleasant aspects of our circumstances such as loneliness and boredom. Simultaneously, we yearn to pursue moments of pleasure and comfort.

This duality of human behavior is ingrained within us, yet the teachings of Eastern philosophy and mindfulness encourage us to transcend these impulses. By cultivating a state of equanimity and inner peace, we can navigate the ups and downs of life with grace and resilience. Embracing solitude becomes an opportunity for self-discovery, inner growth, and ultimately, liberation from the endless cycle of desires and fears.

Redefining Priorities: Reflections on Survival and Self-Actualization

Remember the initial goal? Locking ourselves away to protect humanity. In those early weeks, as the severity of the virus was still unknown, survival mode kicked in. We experienced a taste of life before smartphones and modern comforts, where survival was paramount and self-actualization took a backseat. When faced with the basic need for food and shelter, concerns about boredom or relationship status became insignificant. Our sole focus was on survival, a mindset ingrained in us for centuries.

Fast forward to today, and we live in an era of relative security. Our survival is often ensured by support systems like family, government, or social safety nets. With the essentials taken care of, our attention turns inward. We become consumed by thoughts of self: "I'm bored at work," "I'm alone," "I'm out of shape," "I don't know what to do with my life." It's a pervasive "me, me, me" mentality, dominating our thoughts and actions.

Even amidst a global crisis like COVID-19, where the initial response was solidarity and unity, we quickly reverted to a **self-centred** focus as time passed. Our careers, desires, and relationships took precedence once again, but this time with heightened intensity. The pandemic highlighted the tendency to prioritize our individual needs and desires, even in the face of collective challenges.

Individual Beliefs: Empowering Personal Choices

In my journey, I've come to believe in certain principles. However, I don't aim to impose my beliefs on you or convince you to follow my path. What's crucial is that you form your own set of beliefs. The power lies in your ability to choose, to chart your unique course in life. The key is knowing what you want, and once you're clear on that, the possibilities become boundless.

Living Unchained: Embracing Freedom with Core Values

I've determined how I don't want to live my life – not confined, not driven by the fear of judgment. I choose to do what I want, unapologetically. If others disapprove, it doesn't bother me. My belief in freedom extends to allowing others the same liberty. The crux is adhering to a set of core values that guide my actions, preventing me from veering into destructive paths.

Having a clear set of values is crucial for the principles discussed in this book to function. It acts as a safeguard, ensuring I don't end up in undesirable situations. One such core value is the commitment to not harm others while doing what I want. Another cornerstone is the unwavering dedication to seeking the truth, facing life as it is without distortion.

These values define me and underscore the essence of living authentically and freely.

The Journey of Self-Discovery: Embracing Change and Uncovering Values

To truly know yourself, the journey is continuous. People evolve, and committing to a life of growth and freedom means you're not the same person as yesterday. Each day is an opportunity to be different, to embrace change. Unfortunately, some believe in a static existence, claiming, "This is simply who I am." That perspective, to me, is pessimistic.

From my viewpoint, I acknowledge that I was worse yesterday, weaker, and possessed less knowledge. Why? Because I learn every day, striving to become better continually. If you judge me based on my past, you're judging someone else. Today, I am a new person. Life isn't static; it's a dynamic, unfolding journey.

A common misconception is that we inherently know who we are. The truth is, we must constantly uncover our values. Adopting a static view of life leads people to give up, believing there's nothing they can change. That's a fallacy. Regardless of where you are, you always have the power to do something about it, to decide your course of action.

The key is to know what you want. If you're uncertain, consider reading this book as an exercise to help you discover the way you want to live. Over the past four years, this has been my daily contemplation, leading me to a clear understanding of how I want to live my life.

Finding Purpose: Beyond Selfish Pursuits

Deep down, we all yearn for happiness and a sense of significance. Yet, what's the use of happiness if it's coupled with a feeling of uselessness? The pursuit of happiness, when solely self-serving, may provide temporary satisfaction, but eventually, we realize that life extends beyond our individual desires.

True happiness and usefulness stem from a profound sense of self-worth. However, the challenge arises when we don't truly know who we are. This lack of self-awareness is a prevalent issue, as many fail to consider what truly matters to them. Living consciously requires establishing personal guidelines – our values – to navigate life's complexities.

Understanding ourselves and our desires is an ongoing journey, one that continues until the end of our days. Complete self-knowledge is unattainable, serving as a reminder of the infinite depth within us. Thus, the essence of self-knowledge lies not in reaching a final destination but in embracing the perpetual process of self-discovery and growth.

Empowering Choices: The Role of Core Values in True Freedom

True freedom begins with self-awareness—knowing who you are and what you want. In your life, you hold the reins; it's your decisions that shape your path. No one else should dictate your choices. However, without core values, life can become a tumultuous journey, lacking direction and purpose.

Who are you, and what do you stand for? These are questions only you can answer, defining the essence of your being. The power to decide rests within you, a realization that many overlook. Often, we live under the illusion that obedience to others is our only path. The fear of disappointing those around us becomes a heavy burden.

Yet, this is your life, and feeling good about it is paramount. You don't need constant happiness, but a sense of fulfilment in your actions. Recognizing your power to shape your own narrative is a crucial step toward living a life that resonates with your values and brings genuine satisfaction.

Breaking Free from the 'Funeral Mood': Navigating Mental Wellness

No one deserves to endure a perpetual state of what I refer to as the "funeral mood." This mindset engulfs us when our mental well-being falters. Take a moment to reflect on your own life. Do you find yourself frequently plagued by negative thoughts about yourself? Such a disposition is far from normal.

It's natural to experience occasional fatigue or temporary lows, easily remedied by a good night's sleep. These occurrences may happen a few times a year, but persistent fluctuations in mood are cause for concern. If you find yourself trapped in a cycle of emotional ups and downs, it's crucial to address the root cause and seek support to break free from this detrimental pattern.

Authentic Living: The Power of Inner Battles and True Freedom

I was pleasantly surprised to find that the principles in "Win Your Inner Battles" still hold up remarkably well. Witnessing the long-term effects of this way of life has been truly astonishing. Let me be clear – I'm not one to sugarcoat. The idea of "fake it till you make it" has never resonated with me; honesty and straightforwardness are deeply ingrained in my nature. When I penned this book, I approached it with unwavering honesty and conviction, firmly believing in its content. The paramount lesson I learned was the necessity of addressing your inner struggles before embarking on any life endeavor. This belief has endured, as I remain steadfast in the conviction that mental well-being is the foundation for a fulfilling life.

Amidst the cacophony of life and business advice, the core message remains clear: if you're not mentally fit, achieving external success won't bring true satisfaction. I've encountered numerous individuals – kind, talented, and good – who succumb to depression, a stark reminder that mental health is paramount.

This journey may seem introspective, but the underlying message is far from selfish. As you delve into these pages, my hope is that you recognize the wisdom in these words. By the end of the book, I assure you, the principles I share will resonate as common sense. The knowledge you gain isn't new; it's a reminder of what you already know deep within. Recognizing that your loved ones benefit when you are happy and free underscores the universality of our desires. Your life, your responsibility – this is the essence of true freedom, offering inner satisfaction, peace, and happiness that is unparalleled.

Beyond Talk: A Practical Guide to Real Freedom

In a world saturated with ideas, self-talk, positive thinking, and inspiration, this book stands apart – it's not just talk. Every word is grounded in my own experiences and actions. The goal is clear: by the end of this book, you should have a concrete plan to break free. Even if you already consider yourself free, the aim is to help you become even freer.

Throughout these pages, I share insights on escaping the common traps of modern life. While I don't claim to have all the answers, I promise to reveal everything I've learned about embracing freedom. Living life on your terms is the objective, but let's acknowledge the price tag that comes with it. My commitment is to be brutally honest, for I believe that true freedom requires an acceptance of the unvarnished truth.

I don't mince words about the challenges; I believe in the philosophy that centers on the self. Freedom isn't a cakewalk, and if I were to pretend otherwise, I'd be doing you a disservice. Honesty is the cornerstone of my approach, and I want you to understand that, in the pursuit of freedom, you are solely responsible for yourself. It's a hard truth, but an essential one. If you can embrace this reality, then this book holds the key to unlocking a life lived on your terms.

Breaking the Chains: Liberation from Mental and Real Constraints

Within the confines of our minds and the tangible constraints of life—debt, obligations, responsibilities, and interpersonal ties—we find ourselves ensnared. Yet, these limitations shouldn't be accepted as immutable facts. It's imperative to break free from these entanglements, to transcend mental barriers and overcome the tangible obstacles that bind us. The pursuit of freedom is not just about liberation; it's about maintaining that freedom. Remember, it's never too late to embark on this journey towards a life unrestrained.

Habitual Mastery: The Foundation for a Good Life

Every day, each of us aspires to be a better version of ourselves. Yet, despite this shared desire, why do so many struggle to forge a good life? The answer lies in the absence of a solid foundation of habits that can guide and anchor us. A robust set of good habits acts as a protective shield against the external forces that threaten to divert us from the path we truly desire.

The potential is within you to be that person – consistent, energetic, and intentional. These qualities are attainable through the cultivation of good habits. Ultimately, we all yearn for a good life, and it becomes achievable by consciously building and nurturing positive habits.

Navigating the Journey to Better Habits: A Blueprint for a Fulfilling Life

In the tumult of life, remaining unfazed by the constant pull in various directions becomes a challenging feat. Such a chaotic existence not only impacts our mental health but also impedes the construction of a truly good life. The reality is evident, and you're aware of it – worthwhile pursuits demand dedicated time and energy.

Consider the pursuit of physical fitness – a consistent commitment to regular exercise, a balanced diet, and steering clear of detrimental habits like excessive alcohol and fast food consumption. A good night's sleep is also non-negotiable. Likewise, cultivating meaningful relationships requires effort and intentional time allocation. Building a successful career demands years of skill development.

The key takeaway is clear: to become something significant, a deliberate and sustained effort towards positive habits is indispensable. This journey to better habits serves as a reliable blueprint for crafting a life that is not just good but truly fulfilling.

Your Best Self: The Power of Unwavering Focus

Becoming the best version of yourself is an attainable goal, and the pathway to achieving this lies in unwavering focus. Each facet of your life, meticulously laid out in the pages of this book, serves as a guide to channel your concentration effectively. Embrace and follow the outlined paths diligently to cultivate the focus needed to unlock your true potential and become the best in every aspect of your life.

About the Author
Sakshi Shyam Chamat

Sakshi Chamat, born in 2004 in Nagpur, Maharashtra, is a prolific writer, author, boxer, compiler, actor, and publisher. With a diverse range of talents, Sakshi has made significant contributions across multiple domains.

As an author, Sakshi has crafted compelling works, including titles such as "Attitude Towards Life" and "Conceptual Thinking," showcasing a deep understanding of life's intricacies. In the role of a compiler, they have played a pivotal part in bringing forth important themes in books like "Self-confidence" and "Love at First Sight."

Sakshi's literary influence extends to collaborations as a co-author in over 60 anthologies, earning them recognition as a leading writer. The Indian Noble Awards 2021 further solidify their position as a notable figure in the creative realm.

Beyond the written word, Sakshi has explored the world of acting, featuring in three short films focused on health awareness. Their visibility spans across various platforms, including social media, websites, Google, Radio Vrishti, Spotify, Pinterest, podcasts, magazines, and newspapers.

Sakshi Chamat's diverse talents converge into a force of creativity and impact, embodying the spirit of a multifaceted individual leaving an indelible mark on the creative landscape.

9 789395 083195

Printed at Repro India Ltd.